# PEACEMAN

# PEACEMAN

By
MAJOR J. J. DUFFY

Boston
BRANDEN PRESS
Publishers

© Copyright, 1976, by Branden Press, Inc.
Library of Congress Catalog Card Number 76-7118
ISBN 1-4392-6287-x
Printed in the United States of America

ns
## AUTOBIOGRAPHICAL POEM

## SOLDIER'S ODYSSEY

Not too many years ago,
   Off to war I did go,
To do my glory deeds,
   Perhaps to meet my fate.

It was all new to me:
   I knew not yet my strength,
I had yet to brave my fear,
   To meet my foe and not turn.

It all seemed so easy:
   To talk on the radio,
To charge an ambush,
   To kill another man.

That was the beginning;
   Before my comrades fell,
While I still believed,
   It would never be me.

I perceived the truth slowly,
   That I too could be killed.
That all the others thought
   They would not find their end.

I fought on even then,
   Thinking it was my fate,
Watching the others die —
   Awaiting my last moment.

The war has now ended.
   And I who fought so long,
I look back on the past;
   Finally I understand.

## CONTENTS

**PART I – PEACE**
| | |
|---|---|
| Johnnie Walker | 13 |
| Contradiction | 14 |
| War Generals | 15 |
| Blue Chip Control | 16 |
| Shame | 17 |
| Birds of Death | 18 |
| Beat the Drums! | 19 |
| The Anger | 20 |
| A Step | 21 |
| 15 August 1973 | 22 |
| Drifting | 23 |
| Next War | 24 |

**PART II – MAN**
| | |
|---|---|
| Women of the Orient | 27 |
| Siam Songs | 28 |
| Love Dance | 29 |
| Beach People | 30 |
| Francois | 31 |
| Cool Grapes | 32 |
| Pattaya | 33 |
| Cambode Girl | 34 |
| Pattaya Beach | 35 |
| Monsoon Girl | 36 |
| Limpid Lust | 37 |
| Buddha's Delight | 38 |

**PART III – COMPROMISE**
| | |
|---|---|
| Where Else? | 41 |
| Life Question | 42 |
| Death's Credo | 43 |
| Life's Measure | 44 |
| Existing | 45 |
| Philosophy of the Half-Moon | 46 |
| The Vanguard | 47 |
| Momentum | 48 |
| Pity | 49 |
| Philosophy of the Full Moon | 50 |
| Mind Free | 51 |
| Living | 52 |
| Downs and Ups | 53 |
| Impressions | 54 |

Part I

PEACE

## JOHNNIE WALKER

Friend Johnnie Walker:
"Be my companion,
Stay up late this night:
Loosen my deep thoughts."

Allow me freedom,
To write of the times,
And life's flowing ways;
Help me with the truth.

## CONTRADICTION

The bombs are still falling,
   Now from over the Khmer.
They rain terror below
   From high in the clear sky.

Who directs the bombing,
   And why must we do so?
To protect which frontier,
   To liberate what man?

Flying high in the sky,
   Releasing death's birds of prey;
A flash, and dust rising:
   From somewhere far below.

The screaming villagers,
   Bleeding and bewildered,
Torn and broken; and dead,
   Amidst the settling dust.

The President proclaims loudly:
   "With respect and honor,"
While toasting with Brezhnev,
   And smiling at Chairman Mao.

## WAR GENERALS

In the last war headquarters,
All the Generals I did see.
Each morning they would be seated,
As I briefed the current war.

They talked softly — surely knowing
That their orders were carried out:
Commanding brave soldiers to kill
From the sky above Cambodia.

Knowing they would fly their missions:
Dropping their bombs from high above,
Occasionally seeing dust rising,
Never seeing the shadow of death.

But the Generals should have known
And been more wise in their pursuit,
Instead of counting sorties flown,
And tallying innocents killed.

## BLUE CHIP CONTROL

The control center of the effort;
Mounted in an unreal atmosphere,
Almost suspended over man's fate,
Dealing in real time and life's numbers.

Keeping the planes flying through the day,
Directing where the bombs will destroy.
The moments tick by for those below:
Death's decisions are made from above.

# SHAME

So ashamed before
  I have never been,
Watching my country
  Perform manslaughter.

Disregarding the will
  Of this once great land,
Against the Congress,
  The President acts.

The planes fly each day,
  With their deadly loads,
Dropping death's message:
  Aid from the U.S.A.

## BIRDS OF DEATH

The bomber pilots fly at night,
 Dropping their loads from on high,
Never witnessing death's load:
 The agony they deliver.

In the daytime the ground is seen
 From ten thousand feet above,
Before the Fastmovers roll in,
 With their destructive loads.

Pilots flying their missions,
 They drink their nights away,
Questioning sometimes what they do,
 When they fly their birds of death.

# BEAT THE DRUMS!

Beat the drums! Beat the drums!
Manslaughter has been done.
Bombs have been dropped from high,
Raining death's moment below.

The people of Cambodia
Now mourn their lost sons:
Killed and maimed in this war
Which has ravaged their land.

Each drumbeat comes louder;
As the planes fly above,
Drowning out the drumbeats;
Until tomorrow dawns.

## THE ANGER

More than angry am I,
This much I acknowledge,
My country I am shamed,
For killing without thought.

Following someone's orders,
Doing the duty I saw,
Believing others thought;
For we were righteous once.

This will no longer be.
I have seen we kill blindly,
Seeking our own rewards,
Thinking not of the dead.

## A STEP

Can no one say "No!",
Must we all comply
With what we know is wrong —
  Killing other men?

We do not know why
  We do these cruel deeds:
Women and children
  Sent to early graves.

The coldness of it all;
  Press a button now,
Write a word for death —
  This causes me to question.

Where is our courage?
  Do we forget God's hymns?
I see no more myths —
  I must step forward.

## AUGUST 15, 1973

All the years are gone:
   The last has now come.
This war is ended.
   The killing has stopped.

It seems much too much
   We have given for nothing,
Backing off each time,
   Talking our false tales.

I knew too many
   Who died for falseness,
Believing their wish,
   Finding bitter ends.

Where can I turn,
   To whom should I bow?
I have no more respect
   For my beliefs of old.

# DRIFTING

Where are the flowers?
   All the years gone by,
Not one blossom recalled.
   There must have been a few.

All those other things
   I do remember;
The explosions of flame,
   The killing, and death.

Too many innocents
   Were turned to earth.
But where are the flowers?
   These I must recall!

## NEXT WAR

When the next war comes,
  They can find another
To do their killing,
  I have done enough for one.

I will kill no more:
  Doing deeds of glory
For a new Caesar —
  Believing foolishly . . .

That I killed my foe.
  I didn't know the truth,
And that I did kill
  But other fools like me.

# Part II

# MAN

## WOMEN OF THE ORIENT

I like to watch their faces,
These girls of the Orient.
It is like watching history,
To read the stories in their faces.

The Orient has known much
Of man's intermingling.
The girls, it is easy to see,
Reflect what has passed before.

One slender and youthful,
Another blooming in fullness,
This one looking of intrigues,
The last a rogue from the past.

There is something different
In the way of these women.
They seem more sure of themselves:
Accepting life's dictates with grace.

## SIAM SONGS

I do not know her yet,
  But she warms my soul
With her clear singing,
  Reaching within life.

Perhaps we'll soon meet,
  And share a moment.
She sings of romance,
  I think of love's touch.

## LOVE DANCE

The night's last dance,
  We made love in.
She giving freely,
  I wanting her.

It excited me.
  She knew that was so.
Soon we must leave,
  And touch our toes.

## BEACH PEOPLE

Beach people are more free.
 They find their life not tiring,
Always but a frolic away
 In the waters so deep.

Perhaps it is the expanse
 Of so much that is beyond,
That allows them to see
 That all is not important.

# FRANCOIS

A young girl from Paris,
Visiting the beach of Siam.
A chance encounter one night,
Talking and being together.

She pretty and petite,
Now wandering alone.
Her mind and nature strong,
She moves toward romance.

This I do like of her,
That she reaches out for life,
Moving at her own pace—
Finding me to share a night.

## COOL GRAPES

It was new and exciting,
  Together for the first time.
We had traveled a long way,
  To a bed by the sea.

Before we went to bed,
  We walked along the beach,
And bought some cool grapes,
  For that night's delights.

So long and so often,
  We did that night love,
Holding and not letting go,
  While we liked it so.

## PATTAYA

Crickets performing in concert,
   As the sun sets over the Gulf.
At this place, so far away,
   Where I have travelled to hear the quiet.

Fishing boats sailing into darkness,
   Soon to catch their night's haul.
The sound of waves lapping,
   Heard at this restaurant on the beach.

Soft classical music plays,
   The atmosphere is sedate.
An artist-traveler owns this place,
   His paintings reflect his wandering.

I am the first patron this night,
   Others soon sit down to dine.
The wine is cool and refreshing.
   The food is to be enjoyed.

I will be off to a dancing place,
   Where the music plays too loud.
The women, they will move too much.
   This night, I will seek loving heat.

## CAMBODE GIRL

I met her on the street;
    She smiled at me so sweet.
This girl dressed all in black,
    Her teeth flashing joys to come.

I laughed at her beauty.
    Soon we were holding hands.
To a club by the sea,
    We went to drink and dance.

Together our bodies moved,
    Catching the rhythm,
Finding the night's mood:
    Feeling of love to come.

I took her to my bed.
    We undressed each other,
And began the last dance:
    Moving to our pleasure.

## PATTAYA BEACH

This beach resort I like,
   On the Gulf of Siam;
Palm trees and horses,
   Elephants and sails.

What a delightful place,
   Where a frolic is near,
In the arms of a woman,
   Or in the depths of the sea.

## MONSOON GIRL

Dark-skinned girl,
Diving into the pool,
Looking too strong
For a girl so young.

I smile invitingly:
She sits and we talk,
Soon drinking a beer,
And swimming together.

The sky darkens quickly,
The winds start to blow,
The clouds roll low.
Soon, the rain will fall.

I invite this girl
To come with me.
Together we shower,
Washing each other.

Soon we kiss warmly . . .
I taking her in hand.
She making love to me . . .
To the rhythm of the rain.

## LIMPID LUST

We now lay together,
Wasted and lustless.
The pleasures but thoughts,
The smiles even relaxing.

Her nail runs down my back,
The senses do that like.
Her kisses become warm,
My limpid lust is gone.

## BUDDHA'S DELIGHT

Buddha has been corrupted:
The Thais bring him gold,
But the Americans have discovered
His most pleasant delight.

Each night, they leave him
A Mai Tai tasting sweet.
He empties his great goblet,
Before clapping his hands.

His countenance brightens,
His smile enlarges,
His beams radiate,
Before he drops off to sleep . . .

# Part III

# COMPROMISE

## WHERE ELSE?

We are here to create!
We are here to find beauty!
We are here to learn the mysteries!
We are here to pass on our seed!

We are here to study the truth!
We are here to seek life's joys!
We are here to show compassion!
Where else can we sojourn?

## LIFE QUESTION

There is nothing permanent on earth;
No building, no monument, nothing.
Even the ideas of men change,
Philosophers pass, and religions fade.

In life's history, we are but a flicker.
How can we orientate ourselves
On this moment; not allowing it to flash by,
To find the meaning which must be there?

## DEATH'S CREDO

Death is in the future,
No one can escape it.
Life's signs will fade
And decay will set in.

Where do we travel then,
To which God's paradise?
What dreams can be conjured
To allow us to suffer life?

Perhaps the truth is,
That in death, we lie:
Dead and no more —
Happy, resting at last.

## LIFE'S MEASURE

Have you learned life's measure?
  Do you know the worth of your time?
Allow no one else to waste
  This, your narrowing time span!

I know of only one thing
  Which will never return.
That is the time of now,
  Once gone, never again seen.

## EXISTING

Most people exist.
 That does seem enough
For them, in their time,
 To seek the simple ways.

They do not wish conflict,
 Or anything else to disturb.
It must be enough for them
 To do no more than exist.

## PHILOSOPHY OF THE HALF-MOON

To be a King is to be nothing.
 To be hungry is to live of life.
The moment all can be held,
 Is the moment of the eclipse.

A reaching beyond is needed.
 It matters not what is sought,
Only that it never be taken;
 Otherwise, the end will begin.

## THE VANGUARD

How many people are willing
To dance with the wheel of fate?
How many will watch the wheel
Spin between dark and light?

This game, few are willing to play:
The chances of winning are few.
It takes a special compulsion,
To motivate man against the Gods.

But there will always be a few,
Who must reach toward the fire:
Seeking not flame, but the sparkle —
Riding in their own chariots.

## MOMENTUM

Lingering is not for me.
  I wish to stay in motion,
Stopping when I like,
  For what interests me.

Finding of love's moments,
  Seeing the mood of life,
Feeling it passes me not,
  For I will reach out.

## PITY

I was thinking,
  I should sail a ship
Around the world.
  Then I remembered.

Once I did try
  To sail a ship.
The wind blew not;
  I did not go far.

## PHILOSOPHY OF THE FULL MOON

Perhaps it is not one faith
   Which allows one to survive,
But the ability to change:
   Taking life's bends in stride.

To be able to abide
   By any man's philosophy,
Not to fall into blindness,
   Seeing but one true path.

Is this not the strength
   Of man's many beliefs?
Fanatics are forgotten,
   Or soon swallowed up.

The men of the times
   Must learn the new trends,
Taking much from the past,
   Welding it to the future.

## MIND FREE

This is the age of computers.
This is the age of push buttons.
All these things we do have,
But somehow, we have not.

We seek more than before,
Saddening much quicker now.
Simple things of the past,
No longer seem enough.

Now, we must think of all,
Frustrating our sad greed,
Seeking of false delights,
Losing our happiness.

## LIVING

People do not know how to live.
All the time wasted deciding;
How is it best for one to live;
When it is best to love and live.

## DOWNS AND UPS

The rollercoaster of life
  Does rolick through the years,
Sometimes more up than down,
  Sometimes even seeming to slow.

As the years spin past,
  We seem to seek a plateau.
Perhaps as high as we can go,
  Without tumbling back down again.

## IMPRESSIONS

Black dog in white snow,
  Romping over newness.
Watching that even dogs
  Leave behind impressions.